UNDER THE MANGO TREE

by **Carmen Rivera**

STEELE SPRING
STAGE RIGHTS

www.stagerights.com

UNDER THE MANGO TREE

For all stage performance inquiries, please contact:

STEELE SPRING
STAGE RIGHTS

Steele Spring Stage Rights
3845 Cazador Street
Los Angeles, CA 90065
(323) 739-0413
www.stagerights.com

AUTHOR'S NOTE

Although the events in *Under the Mango Tree* are fictional, the grandmother portrayed in the story is inspired by my grandmother's life.

In writing this play, I had the opportunity to really explore my own family history and the various mythologies that had been passed down. I recorded an oral history of my grandmother— which was both a wonderful and painful experience. She was excited to recount her life— which was actually quite difficult. She was orphaned at an early age and had to marry someone much older than her when she was in her mid-teen years to help support her younger siblings. She was very open about her life— with the exception of what happened to the man she truly loved. After the much older husband passed away, she met the man who would become the love of her life. One of the many rumors about my grandmother was that she caught her great love with another woman and then chased them out of the house with a machete in hand— hurting both of them. No one in my family would ever confirm or deny the rumors and my grandmother denied the story until the day she passed on. No one ever knew the truth. I'm sure that incident caused her so much pain, but as a playwright, stories like these are gold. I had license to create a fictional story around the rumors. *Under the Mango Tree* evolved as a love letter to my grandmother.

After that incident, my grandmother became one of the many thousands of Puerto Ricans that migrated to the United States in search of work. She created a new life for herself and my family in New York City. Working on *Under the Mango Tree* has truly been a labor of love. I feel very blessed to have been able to discover my own family history through this process.

I would like to thank Max Ferrá and the INTAR Hispanic American Arts Center for nurturing this play. I would also like to thank Rob Urbinati at the Queens Theatre in the Park, María Helan, Cándido Tirado, Thuy Dancik, my mother Juana Carrero and my grandmother Paula González.

Carmen Rivera
November 16, 2016

UNDER the MANGO TREE

PRODUCTION HISTORY

Under the Mango Tree began as a monologue, entitled *a kiss at the mango tree*, about a young girl's first kiss in Puerto Rico. This monologue was performed in the series "Playwrights in Performance" at Aaron Davis Hall, in New York City. Shortly after performing the monologue, I received two grants to develop it into a full-length play, through the INTAR Hispanic American Arts Center and *Under the Mango Tree* was born, where it received a workshop production in March of 2002.

I have since had several readings of this play, including Women's Project Theatre and most recently at Queens Theatre in the Park, in a reading series curated by Rob Urbinati and directed by Cándido Tirado.

ORIGINAL CAST — WORKSHOP PRODUCTION AT INTAR

Lena: Melissa Delaney del Valle

Fela: María Cellario

Gloria: Nikaury Rodríguez

Belén: Marilyn Torres

Junior: José Sonera

Felix: Carlos Molina

Director: Max Ferrá

UNDER the MANGO TREE

CAST OF CHARACTERS

Cast Total: 4F — 2M

LENA: 12 years old. Angry tomboy.

FELA: 50s. Lena's grandmother. A widow. Reserved, bitter, resentful.

GLORIA: 15 years old. Lena's cousin. Prissy, restless.

BELEN: 50s. Fela's best friend. Very extroverted, jovial.

JUNIOR: 13 years old. Belen's grandson. Funny, curious, a little lonely.

FELIX: 50s. Fela's suitor. Polite, charming

Note: Fela has a pain in one leg— she frequently rubs her thigh and/or knee. Fela and Belen frequently carry fans with them.

SET

Although the play is realistic, I would like the set to be designed in a minimalist fashion. The action takes place in the backyard of Fela's house. There is a mango tree separating her house from Felix's house. His backyard will not be seen, but there should be enough room on his side of the stage for actors to interact.

The scenes in this play overlap. The entire action takes place in mountains of Puerto Rico, in the patio behind Fela's house.

RUN TIME

2 hours.

A NOTE ABOUT THE SCRIPT

Stage directions preceded by asterisks (*), and especially those referencing the mango tree, should be considered very important to the meaning of the play.

ACT I

SCENE 1

TIME: EARLY MORNING

A young girl is playing basketball by herself.

LENA: Five seconds to go in the fourth quarter and the Liberty are down by two points... if they hit a three-point shot they will take the WNBA championship... there goes Lena Ramirez... she dribbles left, she dribbles right... she stops... *(she fakes a pass)* Oh no, she didn't pass the ball, she looks at the basket, she's gonna go for the three pointer...

FELA (O.S.): Stop bouncing the ball, it's too early.

> *LENA gets distracted and doesn't shoot. She gets into position again.*

LENA: ...She aims, 3 seconds, 2 seconds, she shoots... AND SCORES... AN UNBELIEVEABLE SHOT... LENA RAMIREZ WINS THE CHAMPIONSHIP FOR THE LIBERTY!!

FELA (O.S.): I said stop bouncing the ball!

> *LENA ignores FELA. Lena cheers as the crowd in Madison Square Garden.*

LENA: YEAH!!! YEAH!! LENA!! LENA!!

> *LENA runs in a circle in a victory dance for a couple of beats, then shoots one more time.*

FELA (O.S.): What did I tell you Lena?!! Stop bouncing the ball!!

> *LENA puts the ball down and sits down.*

LENA: Man, I can't do anything here! How am I supposed to play basketball without bouncing a ball?! Huh? I bet she doesn't have an answer for that. I've been in Puerto Rico for two days and I hate it. I was supposed to go to basketball camp and instead I'm stuck in the mountains. My mother said I was going to have fun with Abuela, sleeping with her in her bed with a huge mosquito net that looks like a coffin in the dark. Yeah right! That's a lot of fun! Can't walk around the mountains by myself; can't go to the store by myself; can't watch TV too late— she won't take me to the beach... I think I'm gonna die of boredom. And the only person I see is Gloria. I can't believe she's my cousin— there's no way we're from the same family! AND I can't believe I have to be here the whole summer. I hate being 12 years old!! When I am a grown-up, I'm not gonna let anybody tell me what to do.

> *FELA enters the patio.*

FELA: Ah dios mio, watch the roses!! Ya with the ball! If you kill my roses you're going to be more dead than the squashed flowers. I don't know why your mother sent you down here with that... that... thing.

LENA: It's a hoop, Abuela.

FELA: Hoop, ni hoop. Gloria! Get out here.

GLORIA enters, combing her hair.

Are you still combing your hair? It's gonna fall out one day— let's see how many guys want to go out with you when you're bald. Ah Dios!! Oye look at the canisters...

FELA notices canisters of water.

You didn't pour the water yet!

LENA: I thought you just said bring them up from the driveway.

FELA: Look at you two... your parents spoil you rotten like the mangoes on that tree. Vamos, pour the water in the drum.

Both girls pour the water into the drum.

GLORIA: Three months, no rain— it's like some big record.

LENA: I can't wait to take a long hot shower when I get home.

FELA: Will you two stop complaining!

LENA: Yeah, but the latrine is disgusting.

FELA: That's how people been going to the bathroom for thousands of years!

DOÑA BELEN enters very excitedly.

BELEN: Oh my god Fela... Fela, wait until I tell you... Ah... *(taken by surprise)* ...AH... Hello... Buenos dias niñas.

LENA & GLORIA: Hi, Doña Belen.

FELA: Mira, we just got the water. They left the canisters by the road where anybody can take them. Sánganos!

BELEN: You always worry about everything. Oh, when I was a little girl... I used to love when the water truck made deliveries— that was before showers y todo. Everyone in the neighborhood came out and talked and the little kids would run after the truck... AHH... SO Lena, te gusta a Puerto Rico?

LENA: I don't speak Spanish that good. I take it in school but I don't really understand it.

BELEN: Just like my grandson, he doesn't understand papas. Junior's having some problems with friends over there. You know, the kids run around wild in New York.

FELA: I don't know what they do to the kids over there. Esta was getting into fights in school.

LENA: That's not true.

FELA: Don't talk back to me, do you understand? And I'm gonna straighten you out by the time you go back to New York.

BELEN: Junior's coming later this week to visit for the summer. My daughter says all he wants to do is play basketball.

GLORIA: Oh my god, just like Lena— as soon as she got here, she put up the hoop and bounce and bounce...

FELA: Sh!! You speak when you're spoken to.

BELEN: My grandmother used to say, "Children should only speak when chickens shit!"

FELA: Back then children knew their place. And young girls didn't go around playing basketball. Mira, she even plays on a school team... basketball?!

BELEN: It's good for girls to be good at the boy things.

FELA: Naah! She's wasting her time.

BELEN: Pues... I asked you— How do you like Puerto Rico?

LENA: It's nice.

BELEN: Una mierda mija— that what it is... Ai this drought is killing me! I can't wait for the rains... On the news this morning— they said even the hotels are having problems with the water. The tourists must be mad, you know, they take five showers a day.

FELA: Ai, and my leg has been bothering me for weeks. When it does, it usually means that it's going to rain. But nada. Mira look at my garden... all my peppers and tomatoes have died. I tried to keep them alive but... the sun is too hot.

BELEN: You know your roses look so nice.

FELA: A miracle.

BELEN: Mira I heard a story about a lake by Ciales. This jibaro goes fishing and he takes his boat out onto the middle of the lake... he sees something, he gets closer and it's a cross.

Imagínate! The whole town went crazy. They probably thought that Jesus was coming or something. A miracle!! People were coming from all over to pray; they were going in the water... you know to bathe in holy water. Somebody even said the Pope was gonna come and bless the town. Well the drought starts to get worse and the lake really starts to dry up and guess what they found? *(pause)* A church. Right there in the middle of the lake. Everybody was so upset— the Pope never went to Ciales. No miracle.

FELA: And nobody knew it was there?

BELEN: Not even the oldest person in town knew about it— and the news said he was 102— mira eso, that church was in the lake for more than a hundred years... They cleaned it up and painted it— and now the people are praying there again.

FELA: Wait until the next rains come.

BELEN: Hey Lena, Puerto Rico is a crazy place huh?

LENA: I guess so.

FELA: Mira we need some bread. You and Lena go to the bodega. And we need some sugar, potatoes— if they don't have any potatoes... get some yucca or some rice, and don't think about going anywhere else.

GLORIA: Yes Abuela. Come on Lena.

FELA: Do not go past the bodega!! You can buy yourself a soda each— but do not go anywhere else. Do you hear me?

GLORIA: Yes.

FELA: And don't talk to the men that hang around the bodega. They're bums— always trying to steal a girl's heart and then they disappear, leaving a girl barefoot and pregnant.

BELEN: Ave Maria Fela!! They're just going to buy food.

FELA: They have to learn about how boys really are. Okay go now.

> *Girls exit. BELEN stares at FELA with a mix of excitement and anxiety— walks over to the edge of the yard.*

BELEN: You have to calm down, tú sabes.

FELA: Naah! Esa Lena, she's a wild horse, she doesn't listen to nobody. Ya verás, I'm going to break her.

BELEN: Fela, oh my god, the news, you're not going to believe it... somebody bought Don Santos' property.

FELA: What?

BELEN: After all these years, I can't believe it. SOLD! Some Puerto Rican from New York, who's moving back to Puerto Rico. That's crazy, all the Puerto Ricans from over there are now coming back. I am sure he has to knock down the house.

FELA: I don't care.

BELEN: What if he wants to knock down the tree?

> *FELA looks for a second then walks away.*

FELA: Good luck! Nobody has been able to knock down that tree. How many times did all the men in town try? Every saw they used cracked in half y el bulldozer, remember? It was going to dig the roots out and as soon as it gets to the tree— the motor just stopped working. If the crazy Nuyorican can do it, good for all of us. Oh my beans, I have to start them. Vamos.

BELEN: Ai Dios— we are in between a sea and an ocean and we have no water. God has a crazy sense of humor verdad?

> *BELEN and FELA exit into house. Cross fade.*

SCENE 2

TIME: EARLY AFTERNOON

GLORIA and LENA re-enter with packages.

GLORIA: Abuela!

LENA picks up the basketball.

Can't you live without that thing?

LENA: Two points!! AH!

LENA is making faces to GLORIA. FELA enters, grabs bag, and checks it. Lena plays basketball throughout the scene.

FELA: Oye, your mother called while you went to the store.

LENA: Okay.

FELA: You're not going to call her back?

LENA: I'll call her later.

FELA: You haven't spoken to her since you got here.

LENA: It's not like I'm at basketball camp or anything.

FELA: What did you say?

LENA: Nothing.

FELA: Now you two behave.

FELA exits into the house.

LENA: God, she's such a pain!

GLORIA: You know, if I have to take care of you, you can't play basketball all day long.

LENA: I don't need a babysitter.

GLORIA: Abuela said I have to make sure you don't get into trouble.

LENA: I'd rather be playing with Rebecca Lobo.

GLORIA: Who?

LENA: Only the best female basketball player ever. My coach got me a try-out for this summer basketball camp, sponsored by WNBA and I got in. Rebecca Lobo was going to be one of the coaches. And my mother takes me out to come here for the summer. She said she would make it up to me by buying me this stupid hoop. Please!

GLORIA: You know the fashion world is just as competitive as sports. I'm in this design program in my high school and our summer project is to design 10 outfits— half casual and half evening wear. One outfit is going to be selected and Miss Puerto Rico will model it at graduation next year. We even have to design the accessories... which I love to do— purses are my specialty... Are you listening to me?

LENA: Ah huh.

GLORIA: No you weren't... You know that kid Junito was staring at you.

LENA: Who?

GLORIA: Junito, his father owns the bodega. He's pretty cute.

LENA: He's probably a jerk.

GLORIA: You don't know that.

LENA: Oh yes I do. I play basketball with a lot of guys in my neighborhood and they're all stupid.

GLORIA: How are you gonna get married then?

LENA: I'm not gonna get married.

GLORIA: What? You have to. Everybody does.

LENA: Not me. You know I found something out in Spanish class... that the same word for handcuff is the same word for wife— esposa.

GLORIA: So what?

LENA: Yeah, so what— I'm not gonna let anybody put any esposas on me.

GLORIA: Oh my god? You're not one of those? You know?

LENA: No I don't know.

GLORIA: Oh come on, everybody knows that the girls that play sports are, you know...

LENA: Come on say it... Les-bi-an.

GLORIA: Yeah...

LENA: That's so stupid.

GLORIA: Do you have a girl coach?

LENA: Yeah.

GLORIA: And...

LENA: And what?

GLORIA: Is she...

LENA: She's got a husband.

GLORIA: That's only one coach. But there are a lot of lesbians in the sports world.

LENA: So what, who cares?!

GLORIA: I don't, I was just asking you know, 'cause you dress like a boy, people might think... Listen, I want to be a fashion designer, and I know in my business there're gonna be a lot of guys, who you know... with plumas right... but please don't be a lesbian. But if you are it's okay.

LENA: Look, I don't like boys and I don't like girls, okay?

GLORIA: Fine, but don't be a nun either.

LENA: What about you? That other guy behind the counter was staring at you.

GLORIA: He's stupid. Big dumb jerk! Mamao!

LENA: Was he your boyfriend...? He was your boyfriend! I guess you're not together anymore, since you didn't talk to him. Did you break up with him or did he break up with you?

GLORIA: Can you believe he always wanted me to watch him play baseball and hold his glove when we were walking home from the baseball games? One day I refused to carry that smelly glove. He got really mad at me and started screaming at me— like I was his wife or something. That was it. Got my purse, I turned around and walked right out of the baseball field. I'm not waiting for nobody. That's why I didn't talk to him. Then he told everybody that I'm conceited and stuck-up— just because I didn't want to carry his glove. I can't wait to get out of here. You know I want to travel the world, go to fashion shows... Next year— when I get my car— FREEDOM!

LENA: Isn't there a movie theatre around here or something?

GLORIA: In town, but Abuela will never let us go alone... guess why? Too many boys. I wish I could go to New York for two months. The counselor in my school told me that there's a big fashion college there. I bet there's a lot of things to do in New York.

LENA: I don't know— hang out with my friends... play basketball... handball... go to the beach... swimming... go to the movies... (she bumps into tree as she shoots the ball) These are strange mangoes huh?

GLORIA: Don't touch them!

LENA: Why?

GLORIA: They're poison.

LENA: Poison? They just look rotten.

> She holds up a mango and smells it. GLORIA grabs the
> mango from her hand and throws it on the ground.

GLORIA: Yuch, uui... I'm not kidding, you can't eat them— the tree is haunted.

LENA: How can a tree be haunted? I've seen a lot of books and movies and there's never a haunted tree.

GLORIA: That tree is... the mangoes just keep growing— dead.

LENA: They look dead, but they're not. They're like Zombie Mangoes.

GLORIA: Even the drought hasn't finished killing them off. Isn't that strange?! And nobody can knock down the tree. That's only possible if there's a spirit in there.

LENA: So who's haunting the tree?

GLORIA: Keep it down! We're not supposed to talk about it... forget I said anything.

LENA: Are you crazy?! Don't leave me hanging...! Who's haunting the tree? Is it the mummy?

GLORIA: Cut it out Lena!

LENA: Just tell me.

GLORIA: You can't tell anyone!

LENA: Who am I gonna tell? There's nobody around here.

GLORIA: I'm serious Lena.

LENA: Okay.

GLORIA: Don Santos, he owned the house. One day, his wife disappears... nobody knows where. Don Santos walked all over town looking for her. But he never found her.

LENA: So, his wife is the spirit?

GLORIA: No, no listen. People in the town said she ran away with another man... other people said she had an affair with a married man from this town— NOW... guess who she was having the affair with?

LENA: I don't know, who?

GLORIA (*whispering*): Abuelo.

LENA: What?

GLORIA: Our grandfather...

LENA: How do you know that?

GLORIA: Everybody in town talks about it... and guess what Abuela did?

LENA: What?

GLORIA: You promised! It's even bigger than what you think. This has to be the biggest secret you ever keep.

LENA: What already?!

GLORIA: The reason why Don Santos couldn't find his wife was because Abuela killed her.

LENA: No way!

GLORIA: Serious.

LENA: I don't believe it. How could she kill somebody?

GLORIA: It's true. Abuelo had this girlfriend— who was Don Santos' wife— and one day Abuela caught them together and...

LENA: Killed her?

GLORIA: And Abuelo.

GLORIA crosses her finger across her throat.

LENA: That is such a lie. Mami heard stories that Abuelo was like Santa Claus. He was really nice. Why would he cheat on Abuela?

GLORIA: It's true.

LENA: Why didn't she go to jail?

GLORIA: Mami said no one in the town ever said a word. Everyone is scared of her.

LENA: My mother never said anything to me about that.

GLORIA: Nobody ever talks about it.

LENA: How do you know?

GLORIA: I was shopping one day with Abuela and Mami— and some lady came up to us and started saying prayers and yelled 'murderer' at her. I was so scared. Abuela never talked about it and Mami said never to say anything again.

LENA: That still doesn't prove anything.

GLORIA: But... everybody in town knows the story.

LENA: That doesn't explain the zombie mangoes.

GLORIA: Don Santos hung himself on the mango tree.

LENA: III!

GLORIA: You can't mess with the spirits Lena. Don Santos comes out of the tree in the middle of the night and he goes looking for his wife. The house stayed empty all these years. Nobody wants to go inside even to clean it— or try to sell— or knock it down. Have you heard the leaves rustling at night? That's the spirit of Don Santos. He comes here every night at the same time. You can almost hear him breathing.

LENA: Man, dead people can't breathe. You're trying to scare me.

GLORIA: He goes near Abuela's bedroom.

> *GLORIA makes the wind sound.*

LENA: Okay, you're freaking me out! Stop it!

> *GLORIA continues making the wind sound.*

GLORIA: Did you see him last night?

LENA: STOP IT GLORIA!

> *LENA pushes GLORIA.*

GLORIA: Don't push me!

> *GLORIA pushes her back.*

FELA (O.S.): What's all the noise?

LENA & GLORIA: Nothing.

FELA: Ah hah... get inside right now and wash up for dinner. Come on, let's go.

> *They exit into house. Lights shift into late evening. Coqui sounds are heard and then the strong sound of wind. "The wind" is heard for a couple of beats.*

SCENE 3

TIME: EARLY MORNING

Lights slowly fade up. FELA enters with a bowl and a bag. She sits down with bowl on her lap.

FELA: Lena... when you finish talking to your mother, come outside.

FELA begins cutting open bean pods. LENA enters, upset.

What did your mother say?

LENA: Nothing.

FELA: What do you mean nothing?

LENA: Nothing... you were the one who wanted me to talk to her so I did.

FELA: You should want to talk to your mother.

LENA: She doesn't say anything. She's just asks me— are you okay? Are you behaving?

FELA: Behaving, hmph... you're lucky I didn't tell your mother what a smart mouth you have. She's got enough to worry about. Did you wash your hands?

LENA: Yes.

FELA: Sit down here... Pues, mira... you gotta open up the bean like this and then all the little gandules slide out... you see... *(she smells them)* I can't believe the bodega had such fresh beans. You try it.

LENA tries it.

No like this...

LENA tries it again.

Better... okay, here.

FELA gives LENA a bowl. There is silence for a couple of beats.

LENA: You know Abuela, I noticed that mango tree, the mangoes look really weird— like grey, green...some are even black.

FELA: Don't eat those mangoes!!

LENA: Fine... um... Well it seems weird that Don Santos' house is abandoned and the mangoes keep growing.

FELA: How do you know about Don Santos?

LENA: Um... I don't know... from around... at... at the bodega.

FELA: Just forget about the whole thing okay? And don't listen to those bochincheros. Did you go on his property?

LENA: No!

FELA: Don't lie to me.

LENA: No, I didn't, I swear.

FELA: Don't swear! Stay away from the house. I don't know why children are always getting into things that are not their business and hurry up! We have more beans to peel. Here's some more.

FELA gives her more beans. Pause.

LENA: Abuela?

FELA: What now?

LENA: Um, Mami said she remembers a little bit about Abuelo and I wanted to know...

FELA: Why do you ask so many questions? Your grandfather's gone. He's gone, okay?

LENA: Gone?

FELA: Yes. Left me alone to raise two daughters all by myself. Oye stop asking so many questions.

BELEN enters pushing JUNIOR— who is holding a basketball.

BELEN: Would you come on...! Ah dios— mangansón!! Fela... Fela...

FELA: Belen.

BELEN: Hello— mira my grandson Junior— say hello to Doña Fela.

JUNIOR: Hi Doña Fela.

BELEN: Say it nicer.

JUNIOR *(a little nicer)*: Hi Doña Fela.

FELA: Hello Junior. This is my grand-daughter Lena.

LENA: Hi.

JUNIOR: Hi. Can I leave now?

BELEN: Oye malcriao— have some respect. You have to wait, young man. He's here one day and he's driving me crazy. Anyway, how are you Fela?

FELA: The same thing.

JUNIOR: I wanna go play basketball.

BELEN: No.

JUNIOR: Why not?

BELEN: Because I said so. OYE— You're only 13 years old— I don't see a beard on your face— so you are not man enough to talk to me like that! If I talked to my grandmother like that she would have smacked my face— then if my mother found out— she would have smacked me too. Then if my tia found out... olvídate— everybody smacks you if you're nasty to adults.

FELA: That's why you have to be tough on the kids...

BELEN: Exactly... Jodón and stop bouncing the ball.

JUNIOR: Whatever!

FELA: So you like basketball?

JUNIOR: Yup— I gonna be bigger than Carmelo Anthony.

BELEN: Ese Carmelo Anthony didn't fail all of his classes and get left back.

JUNIOR: Why you telling people my business?

BELEN: Sigue with that nasty mouth.

FELA: Como esta— and then she's always with the ball.

JUNIOR: You play basketball? Or what, you like to watch it!

> He laughs at his own joke.

LENA: I like to play it.

JUNIOR: What position?

LENA: Forward.

JUNIOR: You're a forward— you're too short!

LENA: Well, I am a forward.

JUNIOR: I'm a guard.

LENA: What, you don't think girls can play basketball?

FELA: Lena! You don't talk to boys like that.

LENA: Fine.

FELA: Belen, do you want some coffee?

BELEN: Ai si...

> BELEN and FELA walk toward the doorway.

You behave— *(to Junior)* I'm right inside.

FELA: Lena, ten cuidado...

> BELEN and FELA enter the house.

JUNIOR: Man, my grandmother is a pain-in-the-ass.

LENA: Tell me about it. I can't do nothing. You know she doesn't let me go to the basketball courts.

JUNIOR: So you're a forward huh?

LENA: Yeah.

JUNIOR: Let's see what you got!

> LENA and JUNIOR play a pick-up game. Lena shoots and scores.

LENA: Two points!

JUNIOR: Not bad.

LENA: What do you mean, not bad?! That went right in.

JUNIOR: Okay, okay... let's go.

> They continue playing.

LENA: Swish... two more points!! Too bad— you're getting beat by a girl!!

JUNIOR: I'm letting you win.

LENA: You don't have to give me anything. I'm taking it. HAH!

She throws the basketball at him.

Come on Lebron James, let's go!!

JUNIOR: Bet!

They play again. LENA becomes aggressive in getting the ball away from JUNIOR.

Watch out!

LENA: Hey that was a foul!

JUNIOR: No it wasn't.

BELEN and FELA enter and surprise the children.

BELEN: See you later Fela... What's going on?

JUNIOR: Nothing. We were just playing basketball.

LENA: Yeah, that's it.

FELA: Did anybody ask you to speak?

BELEN: Hmph!

BELEN approaches JUNIOR menacingly. A man enters Fela's patio.

Who are you?

FELIX: Hi, sorry, I'm looking for 7 Carretera Colón.

BELEN: ...Hm... Fela...

FELIX: Sorry, I'm lost... I thought I was on the right road. I'm looking for 7 Carretera Colón.

He shows a picture of house to BELEN.

This is the house.

FELIX points to Fela's house.

See.

BELEN: Let me see that. *(she takes the picture)* Mira... look at this.

FELIX: Yeah, I just bought this house.

FELA: This house? This is my house.

FELIX: What?! Wait a second. This is your house?!

FELA: That's what I said.

FELIX: That son-of-a... sold me your house.

BELEN: Mijo you can say it— son-of-a-BITCH!

FELA: How could someone sell you my house?

FELIX: It was this agent in San Juan.

He shows her a paper.

See, 7 Carretera Colón... The house in the picture matches your house.

FELA: My house is 11 Carretera Colón. That house is 7 Carretera Colón.

They all look at Don Santos' house. FELIX walks towards fence.

FELIX: Oh my god!

LENA: Don Santos' house.

FELIX: No!

BELEN: Ai dios, so you're the Nuyorican. You can't live in that broken down house.

FELIX: No, no, no... why... why would I... of course, the price was just too good.

FELA: Here, sit.

FELIX: Why would anybody do this? He showed me this picture. And I loved the flowers and this color— like an orange pink. I thought that was unusual in the mountains. I fell in love with the picture.

BELEN *(looking at picture)*: Mira Fela, your house looks good.

FELA: You didn't check the house first?

FELIX: I made all the arrangements from New York.

BELEN: I thought you Nuyoricans were too smart to let someone cheat you.

FELIX: I thought these scams only happen in the US.

BELEN: Oye, wake up m'ijo!

FELIX: I'm not taking this house... I'm tracking this guy down and suing the pants off of him. Unbelievable! Ah... I'm sorry, my name is Felix Plaza.

FELA and FELIX shake hands. There is a very subtle connection.

FELA: Fela.

BELEN: I am Belen! This is my grandson Junior. Say hi, Junior.

JUNIOR: Hi.

BELEN: And Lena.

LENA: Hey.

FELIX: Well, let me get going.

BELEN: Good luck!

FELA: Take care.

FELIX: You take care.

FELIX exits.

BELEN: Mira que cosa.

FELA: That agent should be ashamed of himself. You see Lena, you have to be careful, don't trust business people.

BELEN: Pues, let me go. Come on Junior.

JUNIOR: Can I stay and play for a little while?

BELEN: No.

JUNIOR: Why not?!

BELEN: Don't raise your voice. I said let's go— and I'm not going to say it again.

JUNIOR: See you later Lena...

LENA: Bye.

BELEN and JUNIOR exit.

FELA: I saw how you were playing with Junior.

LENA: I play with boys all the time.

FELA: Well you shouldn't do that. It doesn't look right.

LENA: Who's looking?! There's nobody around.

FELA: It's dangerous. You never know what's in a boy's mind.

LENA: It's just basketball. And I don't like him anyway.

FELA: That doesn't matter. I can't believe your mother lets you play with boys.

LENA: She doesn't care what I do. She's just worried about papi and his girlfriends.

FELA: Don't say that about your mother! She's going through a bad time now. That good-for-nothing father of yours is driving her crazy. I can't wait for her to get rid of him.

LENA: Don't talk about my father!

FELA: If you think you're gonna get away with those malacrianzas... you're in the wrong family.

FELA exits into house— cross fade.

SCENE 4

TIME: MIDDLE OF THE NIGHT

Lights shift... to evening— coquies are heard. The sound of a strong wind blowing is heard.

LENA: That's the strongest wind I ever heard... okay... It's just wind stupid... it's Don Santos... there's no such thing as ghosts... okay... okay, calm down... wow look at the stars.

LENA (CONT'D): There's millions of them. *(closes her eyes)* Make a wish— I wish I was a forward for the New York Liberty and I wish I could go home and I wish my parents loved each other...

> *FELA enters the yard in her robe. She appears to be walking in a trance. The Daniel Santos bolero "If You Loved Me" ("Si Tú Me Quisieras") is heard. LENA carefully moves away from Fela. She realizes that her grandmother doesn't see her.*
>
> *FELA goes over to the mango tree, picks up several mangoes and puts them in her robe and begins to dance as if she were dancing a romantic dance with a partner. She dances for a couple of beats, then twirls— as if she were twirling on a dance floor. LENA freezes then slowly moves away from her and exits through the driveway. Fela remains on stage dancing. The sound of the wind gets stronger then subsides. The sound of coquies are also heard. Cross fade.*

SCENE 5

PLACE: PATIO
TIME: DAY-TIME

> *JUNIOR and LENA are playing basketball— they just shoot baskets while they talk. GLORIA is sketching on a pad.*

LENA: I'm telling you she was picking up the mangoes and was dancing.

JUNIOR: So, let me get this straight— your grandmother sleepwalks, she killed your grandfather and Doña Santos; Don Santos hung himself on the tree; his spirit comes out of the tree every night to look for his wife and the mangoes are poisoned... zombie mangoes.

LENA: Right.

JUNIOR: Cool!

GLORIA: Hey! You two should keep it down.

LENA: Who's gonna hear us, the birds?

GLORIA: Very funny.

JUNIOR: People who sleepwalk are hiding something or something happened to them that was so bad that they can't get over it.

GLORIA: How do you know that?

JUNIOR: My dad's a detective. Usually criminals that feel guilty...

GLORIA: Shut up! Abuela is not a criminal... Lena, we shouldn't have told him anything.

JUNIOR: I'm just trying to help.

LENA: I know she's really mean... but killing somebody— I don't know.

GLORIA: That's true. Hey is that all you two are gonna do all day long?

LENA: What do you think?

JUNIOR: Let's play one on one, okay.

> *He throws the ball to GLORIA. Gloria jumps away from it.*

GLORIA: Get out of here. You're crazy! I can't believe I'm stuck with you kids.

> *LENA grabs ball.*

LENA: Too bad we're stuck with "the beauty queen..." Come on 15...

GLORIA: 15 what?

LENA: NO! First to get 15 points.

> *JUNIOR throws the ball to LENA. They start playing. GLORIA starts to stare at Lena and follows her as she plays. Lena shoots and misses. While the girls talk, Junior checks out the mangoes.*

Get out of the way! You made me miss a shot.

GLORIA: Sooorrry. What's your favorite color?

LENA: Who cares?

GLORIA: How about a yellow sweat suit?

LENA: How about leaving me alone!

> *LENA throws ball to JUNIOR.*

Come on Junior.

JUNIOR: Man, I really love mangoes, I wonder if these mangoes are really poisoned.

LENA: I love mangoes too. *(she picks up a mango)* Only one way to find out.

> *LENA throws a mango to JUNIOR, who catches it.*

Heads up!

> *She throws one to GLORIA, who lets it drop.*

Heads up!

GLORIA: Are you kidding?

LENA: Okay— everybody has to try one at the same time.

GLORIA: I'm not. Lena— they're black... you even call them zombie mangoes.

JUNIOR: Maybe we'll become zombies— then we can talk to the dead and find Don Santos and his wife in HELL...

GLORIA: I'm going home.

LENA: Go then!

> *GLORIA doesn't leave.*

LENA (CONT'D): Leave already. Ah, 'cause you know you have to take care of me.

GLORIA: What am I gonna tell Abuela if you die?

LENA: Nobody is gonna die. Okay— when I count to three we eat the mangoes... Let's see if they're poison.

> *JUNIOR and LENA peel the mangoes. GLORIA closes her eyes.*

1... 2... 3...

> *LENA just takes a little bite, then she spits it out.*

AHH! Yuch!! Gross.

GLORIA: Nooo... Junior didn't eat his... chicken!!

LENA: Ah hah— you're a chicken!

JUNIOR: I wasn't ready.

LENA: Try it... 1... 2... 3... GO!

> *JUNIOR takes one bite.*

JUNIOR: Yuch... You wanna try some...

GLORIA: Stop it!

> *JUNIOR all of a sudden, pretends to choke...*

JUNIOR: Help...

> *JUNIOR continues choking— falls to the ground.*

GLORIA: Lena, do something... AHH!!

JUNIOR: I can't breathe!!

LENA: Junior...

> *JUNIOR gasps for air and then passes out.*

Junior...

GLORIA: Oh my god he's dead.

LENA: No... Junior...

> *LENA pokes him and he doesn't move. All of a sudden— JUNIOR jumps up.*

GLORIA & LENA: AH!

JUNIOR: SIKE!!

LENA: You're a jerk.

> *LENA pushes him down.*

JUNIOR: You thought I died ha, ha, ha...

LENA: No, I didn't. I knew you were faking.

JUNIOR: Gloria thought I died.

GLORIA: You are the stupidest boy I know!!

> *Pause. All of a sudden, LENA walks away, holding her stomach.*

What happened?

> *LENA grabs onto her stomach, then her pants.*

Lena what happened? Stop playing around!

LENA: Oh my god Gloria... I have to go inside.

GLORIA: Lena.

> *LENA runs inside the house. GLORIA and JUNIOR follow her inside. FELA and BELEN enter, returning from shopping.*

BELEN: Can you believe the mayor cancelled the Fiesta of San Lorenzo?

FELA: It's never been cancelled. Since we were little. Even after that big hurricane, remember? Some of the houses on the side of the mountain just slid down and disappeared and we still had the fiesta.

BELEN: All the clowns, food and music... we should pray to San Lorenzo for rain. I heard on the radio today that the government is closing el Yunque. The rain forest is turning brown and somebody could start a fire.

FELA: The only time El Yunque is closed is during a hurricane.

BELEN: I also heard that all the coffee beans are drying up here— so they have to get Colombian coffee beans from Miami to bring to Puerto Rico— que mess!

> *They laugh... pause. FELA rubs her leg.*

Is your leg alright?

FELA: Oh yeah. It's just a little sore, that's all. It's the same pain again... but look at the sky, not a cloud for miles. You know that Lena asked me about Don Santos... She must have heard something.

BELEN: Ai mija... por favor, you have to forget about...

> *GLORIA and JUNIOR enter patio from house.*

GLORIA: Abuela, thank God... something happened to Lena... she locked herself in the bathroom.

FELA: What happened?

BELEN *(to Junior)*: Did you do something to her?

JUNIOR: No.

FELA: What happened?

GLORIA: Um... um... she ate a mango.

FELA: What?

JUNIOR: Big mouth!!

BELEN: You were eating mangoes!! Condenao!! Coño...

BELEN goes after JUNIOR and he runs away from her.

GLORIA: I told her not to. What if the mango really made her sick? She looked a little sick— she was holding her stomach and then started running. I thought she was going to vomit or something.

BELEN: What did I tell you about doing stupid things?

JUNIOR: I didn't do anything.

FELA: Lena, are you okay?

FELA enters the house.

LENA: LEAVE ME ALONE!

BELEN: Junior— you better tell me the truth!

JUNIOR: I swear Abuela— we didn't do anything.

BELEN: Gloria... verdad?

GLORIA: Doña Belen— she just ran inside...

FELA enters the patio.

FELA: Belen it's not the mango... *(whispers)* it's the Woman's Club.

GLORIA: For real?

BELEN: Oh my goodness! Que bien!

JUNIOR: Women's Club?

BELEN: None of your business. Here, take the groceries home.

JUNIOR: Why?

BELEN: Because I said so. Now go.

JUNIOR: What about Lena?

BELEN: Don't you worry about Lena. Go straight home, I won't be long.

JUNIOR exits.

FELA: Lena, you can't hide in the bathroom forever.

LENA: I'm never coming out.

FELA: Ai stop exaggerating... everything is going to be okay. Gloria, go inside and help her.

GLORIA exits into the house.

SCENE 6

TIME: MOMENTS LATER

BELEN and FELA, who is visibly anxious, have remained on the patio.

BELEN: This is a very special day— ah, que bien... It only happens once in your life. Mother Nature is amazing— one minute you're a girl, the next you're a woman.

GLORIA enters.

BELEN: How is she?

GLORIA: She's okay. I think she's a little shocked.

LENA appears in the doorway.

FELA: Lena venga, come out now! Lena!

BELEN: Congratulations m'ija. This is a big day for you Lena. Ai to be young again. Fela! Remember when we were that age? Ay before you know it— *(she snaps)* —you're a vieja and you're getting hot flashes in a drought and not even the big air conditioner at Sears can cool you off.

FELA: Ai verdad.

BELEN: And they have that air conditioning really strong. Lena, you're a lady now.

LENA: I don't wanna be a lady.

FELA: Well you are one.

LENA: I can't believe it's gonna keep coming back month after month after month!

FELA: Didn't your mother tell you about the period?

LENA: Yeah...

GLORIA: Hey Lena, it's okay. You get used to it. Serious, you do. I got mine when I was 12 too. I was the first one of my friends to get it. It was kind of cool, I felt like a grown-up after.

FELA: But you're not grown up yet. I was 14 when mine came, but in my time a woman didn't need a period to be a woman.

BELEN: Fela, mira, when a young woman gets her period, that's it. She's a woman, everything changes.

LENA: When my friend on the basketball team got her period her parents made her quit the team.

FELA: Well, she's growing up and you girls can't go around playing with boys. Women don't have time to play games Lena. I was working washing clothes and cleaning houses by the time I was 10 years old to help my family.

BELEN: Those were the days huh... it's amazing how much the world has changed since we were little. Mira I met my husband in church. Victor and me, we were always looking at each other. Then one day we started walking and ya tú sabes. Now it's so different.

FELA: Don't give the girls any ideas. They're not meeting any husbands for a long time.

LENA: You married that old butcher when you were 14.

FELA: He wasn't that old, 51— now it's not so old... he was really nice.

BELEN: And quiet and shy... your butcher was a good man.

GLORIA: Mami said you used to own a restaurant, right?

FELA: He built it for me, because he loved my cooking and he wanted me to be okay when he died. It wasn't a fancy restaurant. Ay he was very good to me and my family. He taught me how to study animals, which knives to use with the pig or the chicken and which knives to cut bones or nerves or the different parts of the body. Forget about it.

BELEN: It was a little rinconcito— four tables and a counter that's it. Fela made rice and beans and chicken— and pasteles and pernil for Christmas. You were lucky you found the old butcher Fela. Ay Lena... There was this terrible hurricane. It washed away almost the whole town. Tables, chickens, chairs, dead cows, floating in the plaza... my own bed floating right next to the dead cows.

> *FELA thinks about the story. BELEN waits for Fela to continue.*

Her mother drowned trying to save her little brother— he was only six months. Your great-grandmother wasn't found for weeks. The army came into town to clean up and they found her body far away from the house, but the little boy was never found.

FELA: My father loved my mother so much— he stopped eating, working, just sat around the house sitting by the window. I had to start cooking and cleaning. One morning I made him his coffee... I used to leave it on the kitchen table. When he didn't come to drink, I went to check on him and found him dead in his bed. The doctors said he had a heart attack, but he was only 35. At his funeral, the priest told me that everybody in my family suffers from broken hearts. I'm sure he died of a broken heart.

> *FELA gets lost in her thoughts.*

GLORIA: That's when you married the butcher?

FELA: After my father was buried, I waited one week. I washed all our church clothes and made all six of my brothers and sisters get dressed really nice. I knew that the butcher liked me. He always told my mother that I was very pretty and when we went shopping together he always gave my mother an extra chicken leg for free— he said it was for the flaca, to put some meat on her bones. I was really skinny back then. So I dragged of all of my brothers and sisters to the butcher and asked him right there and then— do you like me? He said yes— then I told him "Okay, if you like me, marry me."

GLORIA: Just like that?!

FELA: Yeah!

GLORIA: You weren't scared?

FELA: Not of him. I was scared of my brothers and sisters starving to death— I had to protect them. I didn't have an aunt or uncle or cousin or nothing.

FELA (CONT'D): My parents didn't have any brothers and sisters.

GLORIA: And then the butcher married you?

FELA: The following Sunday in Church... He was happy, I think with all these kids in the house. He was never married and didn't have any children.

LENA: When did you meet Abuelo?

> *FELA snaps back into a bad mood.*

FELA: No more stories. Gloria, you should go home now!!

BELEN: Ai Fela, por favor, we were having a good time.

FELA: It's getting late. Gloria ya... go.

GLORIA: Bye. It's gonna be okay, Lena.

LENA: See you tomorrow.

BELEN: Gloria, wait for me, we walk home together.

> *BELEN hugs LENA. Lena doesn't hug her back.*

I am so happy this happened to you with your family around you. Family is so important. Hasta luego.

LENA: Bye.

FELA: Bye.

> *GLORIA and BELEN exit. LENA and FELA just stare at each other for a couple of beats.*

We should call your mother and tell her what happened.

LENA: I guess so.

FELA: She would want to know about it.

> *LENA just shrugs her shoulders. FELA stares at her.*

I'll make you some tea, okay?

LENA: Okay.

> *FELA and LENA stare at each other and then Fela exits into house.*

This was the most embarrassing day of my life. I can't believe I got my period— in front of Junior. I don't really feel different. I guess I am. I don't know what to feel. I don't want to tell my mother about it. I mean she's not gonna care right now. Ai! That's it. I just want to die. I want the earth to swallow me up, crush me, make into sand and blow me into the universe so that I never have to live another day again.

> *Fade to black.*

SCENE 7

FELIX enters his yard. He looks around. FELA enters her yard with a pitcher and goes to the drum to fill it with water.

FELA: Oh...

FELIX: Uh, excuse me. Good morning, Fela, right?

FELA: Yes.

FELIX: I just wanted to get a look at the view...

BELEN enters.

BELEN: Fela! The water truck isn't coming this week. Que chavienda!! I'm so mad... oh, hola.

FELIX: Hola.

BELEN: Felix, right?

FELIX: Yes.

BELEN: Pues, hola Felix.

FELA: You said no water truck this week?

BELEN: Not this week, that's what the mailman said. Fela, I only have enough water in the drum for a couple of days.

FELA: I was waiting for them all morning.

BELEN: So Felix, did you find that cabron real estate agent?

FELIX: As a matter of fact, I did. It took a while though. He never took my calls.

BELEN: Of course not.

FELIX: According to his secretary, he was always checking out a property. I tracked down his office and waited for him for days. Finally I cornered him down. He had the nerve to tell me he didn't lie to me. Look at this.

FELIX takes out picture of house.

He said the house was in the picture. I can't believe he's completely lying right to my face. I scream at him— where?! Look, right here, in the corner.

They all look at picture.

BELEN: Mira, in the corner, the mango tree was blocking most of the house. You see Fela?

FELA: That wasn't right.

BELEN: Hijo de la gran puta. ("Son-of-a-bitch.")

FELIX: So it's not fraud. Then he even has the nerve to tell me that I got a good deal because someone else offered him more money to buy that broken down shack.

BELEN: Ah mijo, get rid of it and go back to the United States. Why do you want to live here anyway?

FELIX: I'm retired and I tried Arizona and Florida. But it wasn't for me. My son brought his children to Puerto Rico last year on vacation and they loved it. I had never been to Puerto Rico in my life. I used to hear wonderful stories from my grandmother about her childhood here. She made it sound so romantic and beautiful. Like paradise. What little Spanish I know is because of her. I guess I was expecting to find the Puerto Rico she was always talking about.

BELEN: Big surprise huh!

FELIX: I really wanted to have a house for my grandchildren and their children. I had a fantasy about going back to my roots... passing something on. Now I have these two acres.

BELEN: M'ijo take my advice, go back to New York.

FELIX: But my heart is set on Puerto Rico. I was going to sue him. I was so angry, I just wanted to get rid of it all and find a great house, but I do love this view. The mountains are usually green, they're brown now. They're still beautiful. It feels like you're on top of the world. *(to Fela)* You're very lucky to wake up to this every morning.

FELA: Yes.

An uncomfortable moment of connection.

FELIX: Gotta start looking for the contractors... Well, take care of yourselves.

FELA: You too.

BELEN: Good luck.

FELIX: Thanks.

FELIX exits.

BELEN: Mira. I think he's got the hots for you.

FELA: Don't be ridiculous.

BELEN: Oh, yes he does. The amazing view you have here... hm, por favor I felt a little connection there.

FELA: Belen, stop it!

BELEN: What's wrong with you? Many eligible handsome gentlemen have passed by here and you don't give them the time of day.

FELA: I'm not interested in them.

BELEN: Felix is handsome, polite... and he looks like he could still do it.

FELA: Belen!

BELEN: Do it all night long.

FELA: Stop that!

BELEN: Ai mija, you can't keep holding on.

FELA: Belen por favor.

BELEN: Fine. The mailman also told me today that the mayor is bringing an engineer over to the old well behind the church. Maybe there's still water there. You should come with me.

FELA: I don't know.

BELEN: Ai come on already.

FELA: Fine. Let me change.

> *BELEN exits first into the house. FELA just stares at Don Santos' house for a beat, then exits into the house. Lights shift.*

SCENE 8

TIME: DAYTIME

> *LENA, JUNIOR, and GLORIA enter with towels on their shoulders.*

GLORIA: I've never seen that brook so dry before. The one day Abuela lets us go out and we can't do nothing.

LENA: I bet she knew the brook was dry. That's why she let us go.

GLORIA: She's been a lot nicer ever since you got your peri...

LENA: Gloria!

JUNIOR: What?

GLORIA & LENA: Nothing.

LENA: Man, it would have been so cool to just swim.

JUNIOR: It was just like a little... puddle.

LENA: That brook is dried up for sure. We would have dived right into dust. And no limbes either man! I was really looking forward to having those icees.

GLORIA: And Doña Mercedes makes the best limbes... mangos and coconut, tamarindo, cherry... pineapple, guayaba... I didn't know she stopped making them because of the drought.

LENA: What a wasted day!

JUNIOR: Hey Lena, have you seen your grandmother sleepwalking again?

LENA: No. But I just stay in bed now. Sometimes I feel her get up but I am too scared to move. It's creepy, you know.

GLORIA: If I ever saw her sleepwalk I would just scream.

JUNIOR: You're not supposed to do that. You can kill a person.

GLORIA: Shut up!

JUNIOR: Don't tell me to shut up!!

GLORIA: You're such a pain in the ass. SO, what do we do now?

LENA: Heads up...

> *LENA gets the basketball and throws it to him.*

GLORIA: Why did I even ask? What a surprise!

> *GLORIA sits down and takes lip-gloss out of her purse. As they play, JUNIOR trips on a mango. LENA shoots and scores.*

JUNIOR: That doesn't count. I tripped on a mango.

LENA: Yeah right.

> *LENA stares at the tree.*

Gloria... why do you think Don Santos would hang himself on the tree?

GLORIA: Lena... don't.

LENA: Why not throw himself down one of those hills on the side of the mountain?

GLORIA: Lena...

LENA: He hung himself on the tree to be closer to his wife, because... she's... buried around it. That's it!! Wanna go digging?

GLORIA: NO! Lena!

LENA: We shouldn't dig in the front, then Abuela will know.

JUNIOR: Good idea. Let's go on the other side of the fence.

GLORIA: You're crazy— you can't go there!!

LENA: Ready?

> *They stare at the fence.*

JUNIOR: Ready.

> *LENA and JUNIOR jump the fence and start digging on Don Santos' side of the tree.*

GLORIA: Ai dios mio, if Abuela finds out— no, no, forget about Abuela, you should worry about Don Santos. What if his ghost comes out? Huh? I'm running and leaving you guys behind. You wanna go and do something stupid...

JUNIOR: Gloria, if you're not going to help, zip it...

> *Shuffling and digging noises are heard from Don Santos' yard.*

GLORIA: Hey what's going on?

LENA: Ah man, there's a lot of stuff all over the place.

GLORIA: Like what?

JUNIOR: Oh look, here's a watch.

>*They continue talking as they dig.*

LENA: I found a cigarette lighter.

GLORIA: Let me see.

>*They hand over the items to GLORIA, over the fence.*

JUNIOR: Here's a wheel, it's so small, probably from a tricycle.

GLORIA: Nothing valuable.

LENA: Here's a bracelet...

GLORIA: That's mine.

JUNIOR: No way, what if it's a haunted bracelet?

>*GLORIA thinks for a second.*

GLORIA: Well... that's okay.

>*GLORIA takes bracelet and checks it out.*

LENA: Here's a bag.

JUNIOR: Open it.

>*LENA opens it.*

LENA: Oh my God— it's bones!!

>*BLACKOUT.*

END OF ACT I.

ACT II

SCENE 9
PLACE: PATIO
TIMES: SECONDS LATER

GLORIA: Oh my God! Oh my God!!

JUNIOR: She buried them under the tree.

LENA: That can't be.

GLORIA: I don't believe it. Get over here now! HURRY!

> *LENA and JUNIOR jump back into Fela's yard. Junior empties bag— many bones fall out. They start looking through all the bones.*

GLORIA: Let me see!

JUNIOR: Ah man, your grandmother is smart...

LENA: Wow... this has to be a leg bone... look, this is an arm...

JUNIOR: This looks like a rib...

GLORIA: Wait a second... *(she holds up a skull)* This doesn't look like a human skull.

> *They all study the skull.*

It's a dog's skull.

LENA: Yup, it's a dog's skull.

JUNIOR: She killed Don Santos's dog too?

> *JUNIOR looks more carefully.*

GLORIA: No— she didn't kill anybody.

LENA: Just because we didn't find any bones, doesn't mean she didn't kill them.

GLORIA: I know people say Abuela killed that woman and Abuelo— it's different if you find out it's true. Let's just forget about the whole thing.

LENA: You don't want to know what really happened?

GLORIA: ...I... I don't... No, I don't want to know. What are we gonna do? Call the police?

LENA: I want to know the truth.

> *FELIX enters.*

FELIX: Uh... Excuse me, is Doña Fela home?

LENA, JUNIOR, & GLORIA: Ahh!

FELIX: Sorry, I didn't mean to startle you.

> *LENA, JUNIOR, and GLORIA scramble as surreptitiously as possible to hide the things they've found under the tree.*

LENA: That's okay, right...

JUNIOR & GLORIA: Yeah... Right, right... yeah.

LENA: She went into town.

JUNIOR: With my grandmother.

LENA: Yeah— shopping in town.

JUNIOR: They're always together.

FELIX: Do you know when she'll be back?

LENA: No.

GLORIA: Sometimes she goes out all day! All day long! Why don't you come back tomorrow.

FELIX: I actually need to speak to her as soon as possible.

> *BELEN and FELA enter— from shopping.*

LENA: And sometimes they come back faster than you think... you know.

> *BELEN and FELA stare at the children for a beat.*

BELEN: What did you do?

JUNIOR: Nothing.

BELEN: Felix, did these mangansones do something to you?

FELIX: No.

BELEN: Are you sure?

FELIX: Yes.

BELEN: Because my grandson looks like he was up to some trouble.

FELA: Lena? Gloria?

LENA & GLORIA: Nothing— we didn't do anything.

FELIX: Fela, I actually came to ask you something. An engineer was by this morning and there's a problem with a water line.

BELEN: Mijo I'm telling you it's gonna take years to get your house. Y wait until you have to put in the electricity and the gas.

FELIX: Well, the water pipe has to come from somewhere and the family on the other side of me won't allow their property to be dug up so the pipe can be laid down.

BELEN: La familia Diaz was always so cheap! Verdad Fela! They don't share nothing. Remember after the hurricane Hugo?! All the families got together to cook and they wouldn't donate any food. Not one plátano, salvaje!

FELIX: So, the other choice is to have the pipe go through your property. He gave the property a quick check and he thought it might have to go through here. *(points towards tree)* He thinks they might have to knock down the tree to get the pipe through.

Pause.

FELA: Knock down the tree.

FELA says this very coldly.

FELIX: It shouldn't be too much trouble. He said they could knock it down in a day.

FELA: Fine. If you have to knock down the tree then just knock it down.

FELIX: Thank you so much. I'll pay for the damages. I was wondering all morning how I was going solve the problem. I already met with a construction company who is going to knock down the house. Even started making plans to build a new house.

FELA: That's a lot of work.

BELEN: So when all this work is done... will your family be coming down to visit you... son, grandchildren, wife?

FELA: Belen?!

FELIX: It's okay, my son says I should talk about it... I am a widower.

BELEN: Sorry.

FELA: Yes, I am sorry.

FELIX: Thank you. And my family is very excited about the new house.

BELEN: Mijo, be careful when they say... 'tomorrow' y with the drought, 'tomorrow' becomes 'next week.'

FELIX: Thanks for the heads up. See you later.

FELIX exits.

BELEN: He's a widower.

FELA: Ya, Belen... Tell me the truth, what happened?

LENA: Nothing.

BELEN: Junior?

JUNIOR: Like Lena said, nothing.

BELEN: My bones tell me there's something going on with all of you AND my bones are never wrong. Let's go.

BELEN pulls JUNIOR.

If I find out you're up to something stupid... I swear...

BELEN and JUNIOR exit.

FELA: I already told you that IT'S NOT a good idea to play basketball with Junior.

LENA: Why not?

FELA: Because you're a woman now.

LENA: What about all the professional basketball players?!

FELA: Don't argue with me!

In the house, you two... help me with the groceries. Ai my leg is bothering me again.

FELA, GLORIA, and LENA exit into house. Cross fade.

SCENE 10

TIME: EARLY MORNING

Early morning sounds, such as birds, are heard. Then construction sounds such as drilling, chopping of wood, and hammering are also heard. FELIX enters his yard. He remains on his side of the fence for the entire length of the scene.

FELIX: Yeah... just get rid of it. It's not good anymore. Besides I want to clear the yard before the house comes down.

FELA enters her yard.

What a mess! I'm sorry, did I wake you?

FELA: No. I was making coffee.

FELIX: They're knocking down a shed that was in the middle of the yard. I thought I might keep it, but the wood has really rotted.

FELA: That's where Don Santos kept the rabbits.

FELIX: It seems like someone just abandoned it with everything inside of it. The cages, dried out grass— there was some old feed. I'm thinking of extending the house down the hill... They said they could have the whole house down in one week. Something unusual happened though, you know the contractor can't knock down the tree.

FELA *(chuckles to herself)*: Really...

FELIX: He was shocked. It's made out of steel or something. He's gonna get a friend of his to check it out. Actually I was hoping I would see you this morning.

FELA: What?

FELIX: I have good news, uh, this morning, one of the workers told me that the Festival of San Lorenzo is back on. *(uncomfortable pause)* Just wanted to tell you that.

FELA: Really? I thought it was cancelled for sure.

FELIX: Yeah, he thought the town should celebrate anyway. I agree.

FELA: We can't celebrate yet. There's no rain.

FELIX: Might as well celebrate living even without any rain. *(pause)* Is that a cloud?

FELA: I don't think so... no... no such luck.

FELIX: You know I never thought I'd retire. One of my sons took over my furniture store. Had that store for thirty years. He's the one that absolutely loves Puerto Rico.

FELA: How many children do you have?

FELIX: Four sons— no daughters. My poor wife, with all those boys.

FELA: I'm sorry about your wife.

FELIX: Thank you. It's almost a year now... heart attack. One day she's there and one day she's not...

FELA: I know what it's like to lose someone.

FELIX: My sons are good men. I am proud of them. Three are married but my youngest has a new girlfriend every week. How many children do you have?

FELA: Two daughters. One here in Puerto Rico, Lena's mother in New York.

FELIX: I would have liked to have had daughters but I have three granddaughters. They have my heart.

FELA: Granddaughters are tough.

FELIX: Yours seem to be fine young women.

FELA: Thank you.

FELIX: I just can't get over this view. It's really spectacular. You can see valleys on all sides.

FELA: On a clear day you see all the way to the ocean. At night, it's like you can almost touch the stars.

Pause.

FELIX: Did you grow up here?

FELA: Yes.

FELIX: Lucky. I was one of the original Nuyoricans. My family left Puerto Rico way before the big wave in the 50s. Imagine you grow up in a place like this... it's almost paradise. Then you're in New York— no trees, no hills, no fresh air— just concrete and no nature— it's cold and you no longer can see this— *(to the audience)* —from your back door.

FELA: Lena's mother loves New York.

FELIX: My wife and I had a garden in our backyard in the Bronx.

FELA: Imagínate.

FELIX: Yeah. The Bronx is great, a lot of sky. We had peppers, tomatoes, onions, grapes, potatoes, beans and the roses. My wife really took care of her roses. I see your roses look great, you take really good care of them.

FELA: It's been hard during the drought. I also had peppers and yucca— all died. If we don't see rain soon, I don't know...

FELIX: Fela is an unusual name. You don't hear it very often.

FELA: Not so much. When we were young, people were named Guillermina, Espedito, Cresencia, Rosquino.

FELIX: That's true. My mother's name is Hortensia Fernanda.

> *FELA laughs.*

You're lucky it's just Fela.

FELA: It's not really. Fela is short for Felicidad.

FELIX: Felicidad, happiness.

FELA: It's so silly.

FELIX: No that's great. It's better than being named Dolores— full of pain— right? Happiness is better than pain.

FELA: I suppose so.

FELIX: You know I heard... Felix is supposedly another form of "feliz"— happy.

> *FELA moves away from him.*

FELA: I wonder why someone changed it?

FELIX: Who knows? *(pause)* You know, the manager of the construction company... he told me of this wonderful restaurant over by Combate beach.

FELA: Oh, that's far away.

FELIX: He said the food is good. But I hate eating alone. I'm not used to it. Would you like to join me?

FELA: I eat alone all the time. It's better that way. Nobody bothers you.

FELIX: I'm sorry, I didn't mean...

FELA: No... it's...

> *Construction sounds are heard.*

FELIX: Gotta get back to the... you know...

FELA: Okay.

> *FELIX exits. FELA just stares at him— cross fade.*

SCENE 11

TIME: MID-DAY

LENA and JUNIOR are playing basketball. GLORIA is sketching.

GLORIA: I'm almost finished my 10th outfit. My last one is— for New Year's Eve, very formal but chic...

> *GLORIA notices that JUNIOR and LENA are really into their game.*

I feel like I'm talking to a wall.

LENA: 10-9... Beating you!!

JUNIOR: Just by a point.

GLORIA: Not really a wall— more like a fast running river. Sheesh!

> *GLORIA continues sketching. Very loud sound of a wall falling is heard.*

LENA: What was that?

GLORIA: Now, that sounds like a wall.

> *LENA, JUNIOR, and GLORIA run to the fence.*

Yep, look there's just one wall left.

> *Sound of another crash.*

JUNIOR: Not anymore, the whole house is gone.

LENA: What if they were buried in the house? What if the workers find the bodies when they start digging?

JUNIOR: They're not gonna find anything— too many years have passed. Bones are probably dust by now.

GLORIA: Nobody is ever gonna know what really happened.

JUNIOR: There are lots of cases that are never solved.

LENA: Something bad happened if Abuelo just disappeared. There's gotta be some way to find out the truth.

GLORIA: Not now.

> *They all move away from the fence.*

JUNIOR: Hey... weren't you losing?

> *JUNIOR throws basketball to LENA.*

LENA: I don't know what game you're talking about.

> *JUNIOR shoots and scores.*

JUNIOR: Two points.

LENA: I wasn't ready.

JUNIOR: Gotta concentrate and keep your eye on the ball.

LENA: Get out of here...

> *They start playing again.*

JUNIOR: You concentrating... huh? Huh?

LENA: Shut up and play...

JUNIOR: Cause when Lebron James plays he's gotta concentrate with a whole stadium of people screaming.

LENA: Yeah, yeah, keep talking...

> *They continue playing— FELA and BELEN enter. LENA and JUNIOR stop playing.*

BELEN: Oye, you said you were going to be in la cancha, playing with some boys you met.

JUNIOR: They all went home early.

BELEN: Uh, huh.

JUNIOR: So I decided to go home too and then, you know, I passed by here and you know... we started to play basketball.

BELEN: La cancha is on the other side of the way home. I don't like liars.

JUNIOR: I didn't lie, I was at the court.

FELA: Lena, we already talked about basketball, no?

LENA: We were just playing, man!

FELA: Don't raise your voice!

BELEN: Em, vámonos Junior. This better be the last time you lie to me.

JUNIOR: I didn't lie.

> *They begin exiting.*

BELEN: Keep it up. I'm going to give you 100 cocotazos.

> *They exit.*

FELA: Gloria, go home.

GLORIA: But I wanna stay with Lena...

FELA: Go home right now!

> *GLORIA exits.*

This is the last time you disobey me!

LENA: I didn't do anything wrong.

FELA: I told you about playing basketball with boys. But you didn't listen.

LENA: It was just Junior.

FELA: And Junior is a boy.

LENA: So, what am I supposed to do— just sit around and watch the mountains?!

FELA: That's it, give me the ball!

LENA: What?!

FELA: Don't make me say it twice.

LENA doesn't move.

FELA (CONT'D): Give me the basketball!!

LENA: No.

FELA approaches LENA.

FELA: I said give me the ball right NOW!!

LENA gives her the ball.

I'm going to call your mother!

FELA enters the house with basketball.

LENA: Go ahead call my mom!! See if I care! I don't believe this! What she's gonna do with the basketball? ARGH!! How could she do this to me? I was just playing basketball. This is worse than jail... She just hates me and I hate her right back. This is the most terrible place in the world. I'll never come here again, for as long as I live. I wish I could just disappear— disappear like Abuelo. She doesn't have any feelings— I bet you she did kill them!!

Cross fade.

SCENE 12

PLACE: PATIO
TIME: MID-DAY

FELA enters, very upset. She can barely breathe and she rubs her knee periodically. She grabs a mango and throws it over the fence. BELEN enters.

BELEN: Fela...Fela... oye Fela, that was a nice scene you made in the town!

FELA: Leave me alone.

BELEN: You gave all the neighbors a lot to talk about huh? Running after some guy at a bus stop and with your bad leg.

FELA: It was him!!

BELEN: No it wasn't.

FELA is panting hard and tries to hold back tears.

FELA: Didn't you see him by the plaza? And then a bus passed by and he was gone.

BELEN: I saw him too, Fela. It wasn't him!! Ai mija, when is this going to end?

FELA: It was Angel!

BELEN: He's gone, Fela. *(she sits down)* Coño, for a vieja you run really fast.

FELA: What if he's back?

BELEN: HE'S NOT BACK! STOP IT! My goodness! What is wrong with you?!

FELA: Angel never forgave me for marrying the butcher. He never did, he was so jealous of him. He always hated the restaurant because the butcher had built it for me.

BELEN: Angel had a second chance with you. How many people who love each other get a second chance? If he loved you, he would have understood that you did what you had to do. Pero coño he fell in love with somebody else. Tú sabes, Fela, you should really sell this house and move... You should have moved to New York when it all happened.

FELA: What if he's back?

BELEN: He's not back! You're driving yourself crazy... YOU HAVE TO GO ON WITH YOUR LIFE!

FELA: That's easy for you to say.

BELEN is really hurt.

BELEN: That isn't fair, Fela. Do you know what it was like to see the cancer devour my husband? I watched the man I loved disappear and I couldn't do a damn thing about it. This is not a contest about who suffered more. Stop it! What would you do if Angel came back...? Forgive him?

FELA: I just wanted to speak to him one more time.

BELEN: To say what?

FELA: We never said goodbye.

BELEN: Oh I think you did...

FELA: This is none of your business.

BELEN: Excuse me? I was with you throughout the whole thing. Don't you dare tell me it's not my business.

FELA: Por favor Belen! Ya! Go home!

BELEN: Are you throwing me out?

FELA: Would you just go!

BELEN: I don't believe this! You're throwing me out. Esta bien. But you're wrong. You don't know how to let go... you just want to control, control, control... look at what you are doing to that poor girl!

FELA: Lena is my granddaughter. She is my business.

BELEN: That little girl needs you but all you do is give her rules and punishments. Keep doing that and she's never gonna want to see you again. Just like Angel!

FELA: GET OUT!

BELEN: Esta bien. I am so tired of worrying about you, Fela.

BELEN storms out. FELA is left crying. She is left there for several beats as she breaks down. There is a cross fade and the lights shift into the evening. It's as if she was in the patio all evening and into night...

As lights shift, FELA'S mood also shifts... her crying softens— although she is still shaken— and as the wind picks up, her mood shifts into a dream-like state.

SCENE 13

TIME: MIDDLE OF THE NIGHT

The sound of wind blowing is heard. It gets stronger as the lights come up. Daniel Santos' song "If You Loved Me" begins to play softly. FELA is still on the patio and slowly sways to the music. She makes her way over to the mango tree; caresses it. Fela picks up a mango and smells it. It's almost like she tries to dance with the tree. The mango falls out of her hand and she snaps out of the trance. Fela is confused and shocked— she backs away from the tree.

FELA: What...? Angel...? *(she looks around for him)* Angel? *(she realizes that he is not there)* No... no...

She begins crying and runs into the house. Lights shift.

SCENE 14

TIME: A WEEK LATER/MID-DAY

LENA is trying to teach GLORIA how to play basketball— without the basketball.

LENA: Just look at the net— wait... your wrist has to be loose... okay and shoot...

GLORIA tries to shoot and misses.

God you stink at this.

GLORIA: How can I stink? There's no ball.

LENA: Look... *(she takes the imaginary ball, dribbles and shoots)* YEAHHHH... *(she cheers)* You see, to get the ball in, your wrist has to snap like this... *(she demonstrates)* That's why it has to be loose.

GLORIA: I told you a million times I think the game is stupid.

LENA continues playing without the ball.

Lena, come over here.

LENA: What?

GLORIA: Stand still.

GLORIA stands behind LENA...

LENA: What?

GLORIA: Just stand still... now hold your arms out like this.

GLORIA holds her arms out next to LENA'S.

Ah hah...

GLORIA is taking mental notes.

LENA: What are you doing?

GLORIA: Something.

LENA: You're weirder than I thought. Ever since Abuela and Doña Belen had a fight, it's been boring. Like it wasn't boring to begin with. You know what's stupid, that Doña Belen doesn't let Junior come over. It's been a week already.

GLORIA: Why, cause you like him?

LENA: Shut up!

GLORIA: Oh my god you do! You like Junior!

LENA: He's alright, he plays better than you.

GLORIA: Oh my god Lena, your first boyfriend! Okay, so you're going to have to learn to wear make-up and fix your hair differently, Oh, and the clothes have to go.

LENA: No way.

GLORIA: You like him, right?

LENA: Maybe.

GLORIA: Maybe means yes.

LENA: Have you ever kissed a boy?

GLORIA: Yeah. It's okay sometimes and sometimes it feels nice. You know Junior likes you, that's for sure.

LENA: You think so?

GLORIA: Of course. He could be playing basketball in la cancha with all the boys from the neighborhood but he was coming here to play with you... Huh?

LENA: I guess.

GLORIA: You're so silly.

FELA enters.

FELA: Behave, I'm going out.

FELA exits.

LENA: Behave?! What are we gonna do? Suck up too much air?

GLORIA: You're so lucky you live in New York. Imagine— I become a famous fashion designer and you're playing basketball at Madison Square Garden. We both could be famous. Even though I hate basketball I would go see you play.

LENA: That would be cool.

JUNIOR enters with a basketball.

Junior!

GLORIA: You just missed our grandmother...

JUNIOR: I know, I saw her down the road and waited for her to pass. So... um... you wanna play some ball?

GLORIA: Mira Lena, I'm gonna go home.

LENA: No, Gloria... um... Gloria... don't go. You're supposed to stay with me, remember?

GLORIA: My... mother... ah, she said she was going to take me shopping for some material.

LENA: Shopping?

GLORIA: Well... so, good-bye. Good-bye Junior.

GLORIA exits quickly.

LENA: Gloria...

LENA looks at JUNIOR.

Hey...

JUNIOR: So...

JUNIOR throws the ball to LENA.

LENA: Watch out, you don't know who you're messing with.

They start to play basketball. LENA shoots and scores.

JUNIOR: So who taught you how to play basketball?

LENA: My father. He wanted a boy— my first toys were a baseball bat and a glove. I couldn't even keep my head up and he tried to fit the glove in my little hand.

JUNIOR: That's cool.

LENA: I used to play a lot with my father... but we don't play that much anymore. He's got a girlfriend or something. I play with him when I see him.

JUNIOR: That must suck.

LENA: I don't think they should have ever gotten married. The worst part is the screaming. Do you play with your father?

JUNIOR: Yeah... he's always busy though.

LENA: He's has to work all the time?

JUNIOR: Yeah he does.

LENA: You ever see his gun?

JUNIOR: Yeah.

LENA: Ever shoot it?

JUNIOR: No way! *(pause)* Can I tell you something?

LENA: ...Yeah...

JUNIOR: Please don't tell anybody.

LENA: Promise.

JUNIOR: My father killed somebody.

LENA: What?

JUNIOR: Yeah. He was on duty. Chasing a robber. The guy pulled a gun on my father and my father shot him.

LENA: Your father's lucky.

JUNIOR: Yeah, but it turns out the guy didn't have bullets in his gun.

LENA: Oh no.

JUNIOR: He had to stop work for a while. It freaked him out, you know. He's been at home. I think he goes to a therapist or something, but he doesn't talk much anymore. That's why my family thought I should come here. At first I didn't want to come here.

LENA: Me too.

> *JUNIOR dribbles the basketball, stops.*

JUNIOR: I'm glad I came to Puerto Rico.

LENA: Me too.

> *They look at each other and then look away. JUNIOR continues to dribble the ball.*

...What?

> *LENA walks over to mango tree.*

JUNIOR: Nothing...

LENA: I'm sure your father is gonna get better.

JUNIOR: Yeah. That's what my mother says.

> *He keeps looking at her. JUNIOR stops dribbling the ball.*
> *They are by the mango tree.

LENA: What's wrong?

JUNIOR: Nothing.

> *They keep looking at each other. He tilts his head in and softly kisses her on the lips. LENA is stunned.*

LENA: Why did you do that?

JUNIOR: Because I wanted to. Are you mad at me?

LENA: No.

> *JUNIOR leans in again and kisses her softly... FELA enters with a package.*

FELA: Lena!

They both jump up in fright.

LENA: Abuela!

FELA: What are you doing here, Junior?

JUNIOR: I... I...

FELA: I know what you're doing here... I saw what happened... go home and if you ever come back here I'll kill you. You hear me?!

JUNIOR and LENA look at each other. He runs off-stage.

I was only away for a little while and this is what you do!! That's it! I can't take it anymore. I'm calling your mother and sending you back to New York.

LENA: No Abuela!

FELA: Where's Gloria? She's supposed to be watching you!

LENA doesn't answer.

Answer me!!

LENA remains frozen.

You are all so foolish!! What's wrong with you?! You kissed him under the mango tree! You don't know anything about the world!! You're too young to fall in love. You don't know anything about that... women never know anything about love and then they trust the wrong man!!!

FELA catches herself and storms inside the house. Cross fade.

SCENE 15

TIME: EARLY MORNING

LENA remains on stage.

LENA: I can't believe a boy kissed me. I never thought it would happen to me. It wasn't what I thought it was going to be. I mean I don't know, it was nice. In school the boys all like girls that, that look like they're 18 years old already. They're stupid anyway. Junior is really cool. Now I don't want to go back to New York. Why should Abuela care if I kissed a boy? She better not tell my mother. Abuela just keeps making everything worse.

She runs into the house. Cross fade.

SCENE 16

BELEN enters.

BELEN: Fela! Fela, would you please come outside, I want to talk to you.

FELA: What are you doing here?

BELEN: You yelled at my grandson and he was very upset. He said you said you were going to kill him.

FELA: Did he tell you what happened?

BELEN: He just said you threw him out of the house. First me, then him. There's a problem here Fela.

FELA: He kissed Lena.

BELEN: What? AHHH!! Ai bendito, ahh...

FELA: Bendito NOTHING!

BELEN: And what's wrong with my grandson?

FELA: I don't want her messing around with boys!

BELEN: One day she's gonna fall in love.

FELA: Don't tell me how to raise my family!

BELEN: We've been friends for a long time and whatever you feel Angel did to you... you have no right to take out your anger on a young boy. Before you tell me to get out this time— I'm leaving.

BELEN exits. FELA, furious and very nervous...

FELA: Lena! Lena get out here right now!

LENA enters.

I got your plane ticket, you leave tomorrow morning.

LENA: I'm not going to New York. I can go to Gloria's house.

FELA: No you can't.

LENA: Yes I can. I can go right now if I want. Gloria would let me stay with her.

LENA runs away.

FELA: Get back here.

FELA runs to grab her.

LENA: Leave me alone! I'm gonna stay with Gloria.

FELA: No you are not!

FELA reaches and grabs LENA.

LENA: Let me go!! I hate you. I wish you weren't my grandmother.

FELA: How dare you talk to me like that?

LENA: I bet you really killed Abuelo and Doña Santos! *(silence)* Um... I'm sorry, I'm sorry Abuela, I didn't mean it!

FELA: What do you know? What do you know about your Abuelo?

> *LENA doesn't answer.*

You don't know anything! You're worried that you can't play basketball but my life was ruined. You think because you kissed some boy that you know about love!

> *LENA is frozen, afraid to move.*

You don't know anything about love! Do you understand me? NOTHING! YOU ARE LEAVING TOMORROW AND THAT'S IT!!

> *LENA starts crying.*

Lena, stop it... Lena...

LENA: I can't go home...

FELA: That's ridiculous.

LENA: No I really can't— there's no house. They sold it... my parents already got a divorce.

FELA: What?

LENA: It's true.

FELA: Where's your mother living?

LENA: She's staying with a friend until she finds a new apartment.

FELA: Why didn't she tell me?

LENA: She made me promise not to tell you.

FELA: But why?

LENA: She said you would get really upset. I know you think that's good news because you hate my father, but I'm gonna miss him.

FELA: I don't hate him... ay come over here... I can't believe you kept that secret all these weeks.

> *FELA and LENA sit together. She puts her arm around her.*

Mira, grown-ups just make things very difficult.

LENA: Why couldn't they just stop fighting?

FELA: They will now... how can I say this so that you understand... 2 male crabs do not fit in cave.

LENA: That's weird.

FELA: My mother used to say that all the time about women who were very strong. There are some men that cannot get along with very strong women and your father is one of them. That's all.

LENA: So they don't love each other?

FELA: They do. But sometimes love is not enough.

LENA: Is that what happened with Abuelo?

FELA: With Abuelo? Ai mija I don't know— but I know I loved your grandfather very much... (* *she goes over to the mango tree and picks up a mango*) I was always in love with him... ay, since I can remember— we always talked about getting married... In those days people got married at 14, 15, 16 all the time... Then my parents died and I couldn't marry Angel— we were both too young to care for my family, but the butcher could. Angel didn't go to the wedding. He never went to the butcher-shop. When the butcher died five years later he came over to the house and told me we would get married the next day. So we did. *(pause)* That night after we got married he kissed me right under this mango tree. He had this small radio— put it on the patio— and we danced all night. The sky was so clear— the stars were right on top of us and he kissed me as the song "If You Loved Me" played. He sang in my ear as we danced all night. I've never forgotten it... Oh he was so happy when Gloria's mother was born. And when we had your mother, ah... he was the happiest man in the world. He didn't care that he didn't have any sons. He loved his girls more than anything. He used to sing to them at night... He sang all the time even in the restaurant. The customers loved it. (**she tosses the mango over the fence*) Angel would close the restaurant, especially after the girls were born... It was very late one night and your grandfather hadn't come home yet. Your mother— *(to Lena)* —who was just a baby, was already sleeping, and Gloria's mother didn't want to go to sleep. She was only 7. It took a while, but I finally got her to sleep. I heard Angel's voice but he didn't come inside... I went outside and saw him with Dominga— Doña Santos— and I saw them kissing by the mango tree— our mango tree— he was really kissing her— he was kissing her the way he kissed me, I didn't know what to do... I went back inside and waited and waited and waited... he didn't come inside. I kept wondering where Don Santos was... why didn't he stop them? I couldn't believe Dominga, my good friend, was kissing my husband. Then I saw the butcher knife in the sink and I picked it up... I wanted to hurt them— I wanted to kill them... I came outside and they were still by the mango tree and I just started swinging and there was blood everywhere. I heard all of this screaming— Angel was trying to protect Dominga... He didn't even think of me. Somehow he knocked me down and they ran out together. I tried to follow them but I couldn't move and I kept hearing the screaming— it was me, I was screaming. I told him, "If you leave with her, forget about your children. You have no family!!" Don Santos came into the yard, picked me up and brought me inside... I was covered in blood, I had stabbed myself in the leg.

LENA: Your leg...

FELA: Then I fell really hard on the ground and fractured too. I thought Angel would come back but he didn't. I couldn't believe that they just left. Poor Don Santos. We found him hanging on the tree early the next morning. Belen and her husband cut the rope and brought him down. I tried for days to cut down the tree... for weeks and weeks and then months... the tree wouldn't fall and those rotten mangoes kept growing and growing.

LENA: That's why people say they're poison.

FELA: They are— they don't kill you, they don't let you forget.

LENA: Abuela, can I tell you something...

FELA: Of course.

LENA: I saw you sleep-walking at night...

FELA: A priest once told me my family suffered from broken hearts. Ay m'ija, I know I'm tough with you. I was tough with your mother too. My mother once told me you don't know what misery and fear is until you have children. I wanted my children and my grandchildren to be fine, to have everything you want, not to suffer, not to let anyone hurt you, to be respected, to be loved... not to suffer the pain of a broken heart... We should call your mother tonight.

LENA: Okay.

FELA: I love you.

> *They hug.*

LENA: I really didn't mean to say that you...

FELA: Sh... I know...

LENA: I love you Abuela.

SCENE 17

> *LENA is left alone on stage. She pauses for several beats.*

LENA: I am so glad I don't have to keep my secret anymore. I don't know how Abuela did it for all of those years. When I have to write that essay "What I Did This Summer" for school I'm gonna have so much to write about but I can't write about anything that really happened. I can't write about Abuela and Abuelo, that's for sure.

I can't write about the kiss either— oh, and no way am I gonna write about my period. Some things are just meant to be a secret. What am I gonna write about? I can write about Felix and how he's building a house. My parents' divorce, everybody has parents that are divorced... oh and the mangoes— I can write about the zombie mangoes. I don't know if people will believe that though. I can also write about the mountains, the drought... and Gloria and her clothes. I still wish I had gone to basketball camp. I mean Junior is cool and everything but he's not Rebecca Lobo. That's okay though— I'm glad I got to stay with Abuela even though it still hasn't rained. Mami told Abuela about the divorce and the house. Abuela's been really nice to me. She lets Gloria and me go to the town now as much as we want as long as we are back home for dinner. I love her a lot. Mami said we are going to spend next Christmas with Abuela. I can't wait— I really love Puerto Rico.

> *LENA exits. Cross fade.*

SCENE 18

TIME: ONE-WEEK LATER— LATE AFTERNOON

GLORIA enters with a dress in her hand.

GLORIA: Hello I am here! It's Gloria... Hello... Is ANYBODY home?!

FELA enters in her Sunday best.

FELA: Hi Gloria.

GLORIA: I brought something for Lena. I hope she likes it.

FELA: Lena, there's someone here to see you. LENA!!

LENA enters the patio.

GLORIA: Hi Lena.

LENA: Hey.

GLORIA: The dress is for you, Lena, for the Fiesta of San Lorenzo.

LENA: No way.

FELA: You have to go the Fiesta, like a young lady.

LENA: Ah man...

GLORIA: I made it for you.

LENA & FELA: What?

FELA: Let me see.

FELA checks out the dress.

GLORIA: It's my first "GLORIA"!

LENA: You made it... my first dress, now I gotta wear it.

GLORIA: You better.

FELIX enters— he brings flowers with him.

FELIX: Hola...

FELA: Hola Felix.

FELIX: Thank you for inviting me. For you.

He gives her flowers.

FELA: Thank you. They're beautiful... I'm so sorry, I didn't mean to...

FELIX: Don't say anything.

LENA: I forgot something inside... um... let me bring the flowers inside...

LENA enters the house.

Gloria... come on...

GLORIA: But...

LENA: Would you come on already! Help me put on my dress!

GLORIA: Stop bossing me around.

LENA: You're the one that likes to boss people around.

They both exit into the house.

FELIX: You look beautiful. Oh... I have something else for you.

FELIX gives FELA a mango.

FELA: A mango?

FELIX: Strangest thing... You know we couldn't chop down the tree? Some demolition specialist comes over— he hits the tree— the axe nicks it. He tells us the tree is alive. And sure enough the mangoes are fresh. Can you believe it?

FELA: Fresh...? Life is... sometimes... very strange...

FELIX: Telling me— couldn't cut down the tree so I finally had to pay off the Diaz family so that I could lay down the water pipe.

FELA smells the mango. BELEN enters.

BELEN: Look at how handsome my grand... oye where are you? Junior get over here right now!! Junior.

JUNIOR enters dressed in an elegant "white guayabera." It is a dress shirt commonly used in the Caribbean, with four pockets on the front of the shirt.

JUNIOR: I feel stupid.

BELEN: Mira que handsome. I felt bad about punishing him so much so I bought him all these new clothes and a new basketball. He's teaching me to play. Verdad...

BELEN gives him a noogie.

JUNIOR: Yeah, whatever.

FELIX: Junior, you look like a young man.

JUNIOR: Thanks, I guess.

BELEN: Fela, I'm glad you called...

FELA: Sh, sh— m'ija, you're like my sister, I'm sorry.

BELEN: Está bien.

FELA: ...Lena, Lena, Gloria, let's go...

GLORIA enters.

GLORIA: Attention everyone... Lena will be modeling an original "Gloria."

LENA enters with the dress on, but she still wears her sneakers.

BELEN: Oye, look how beautiful you two are. Lena, you're wearing a dress.

LENA: Oh brother.

GLORIA: We have to work on her footwear— pero the dress looks good huh?

JUNIOR: Hi Lena.

FELA: We're all ready. Let's go.

> *They all exit... The wind starts to pick up. Raindrops are heard as lights begin to fade.*

END OF PLAY

UNDER THE MANGO TREE

PROP LIST

- Basketball
- Portable hoop
- Water drum
- Machete
- Flowers — Roses, which form part of Fela's garden (additional flowers can be up to the discretion of the director)
- Bouquet of flowers
- Drawing paper
- Markers
- Coffee mugs (4)
- Water pitcher
- Glasses
- Mangoes — 10-15, depending on budget (director can also choose to mime eating of the mangos)
- Brown paper shopping bags (2-3)
- An old watch
- An old cigarette lighter
- An old tricycle wheel
- An old bracelet
- Small burlap bag
- Dog bones — legs and a skull

SOUND EFFECTS

- A strong wind
- Coqui sounds (a typical frog-like animal from Puerto Rico)
- Song — "If You Loved Me (Si Tú Me Quisieras)" by singer Daniel Santos
- Rain drops
- Rain storm

ABOUT STAGE RIGHTS

Based in Los Angeles and founded in 2000, Stage Rights is one of the foremost independent theatrical publishers in the United States, providing stage performance rights for a wide range of plays and musicals to theater companies, schools, and other producing organizations across the country and internationally. As a licensing agent, Stage Rights is committed to providing each producer the tools they need for financial and artistic success. Stage Rights is dedicated to the future of live theatre, offering special programs that champion new theatrical works.

To view all of our current plays and musicals, visit:

www.stagerights.com

Made in the USA
Columbia, SC
17 December 2017